ADOLPHE-WILLI.

BOUGUEREAU

a book of postcards

POMEGRANATE ARTBOOKS ▪ SAN FRANCISCO

Pomegranate Artbooks
Box 6099
Rohnert Park, CA 94927

Pomegranate Europe Ltd.
Fullbridge House
Maldon, Essex CM9 4LE
England

ISBN 0-87654-365-4
Pomegranate Catalog No. A786

Pomegranate publishes books of
postcards on a wide range of subjects.
Please write to the publisher for more information.

Designed by Elizabeth Key
Printed in Korea

06 05 04 03 02 01 00 99   13 12 11 10 9 8 7

As a young man, French painter Adolphe-William Bouguereau (1825–1905) put himself through the École des Beaux-Arts by keeping books for a wine merchant and coloring lithographic labels for a local grocer. In his spare time, late in the evening, he created drawings from memory. This diligence and discipline resulted in an extraordinarily productive artistic life: he created more than seven hundred finished works and achieved a remarkable level of popular acclaim and financial success. Bouguereau never forgot his difficult early days, however; working secretly, he assisted young artists who were struggling as he had to pursue an artistic career in the face of financial difficulties.

Like many painters of the second half of the nineteenth century, Bouguereau made a careful study of form and technique and steeped himself in classical sculpture and painting. True to his serious and industrious nature, he worked deliberately and meticulously: before beginning a painting, he would master the history of his subject and complete numerous sketches.

The tenderness with which he portrayed children and domestic scenes, his technical skill and passion for the classics, and his love of rich color are hallmarks of Bouguereau's exquisite paintings. This book of postcards presents thirty of his most memorable works. ∎

Adolphe-William Bouguereau
(French, 1825–1905)

Return from the Harvest, 1878
Oil on canvas, 241.3 x 170.2 cm (95 x 67 in.)

Pomegranate Box 6099 Rohnert Park CA 94927

Cummer Museum of Art and Gardens,
Jacksonville, Florida, AP 64.2

ADOLPHE-WILLIAM BOUGUEREAU
(FRENCH, 1825–1905)

Le ravissement de Psyché, 1895
Oil on canvas, 209 x 120 cm (82⁹⁄₃₂ x 47¼ in.)

POMEGRANATE BOX 6099 ROHNERT PARK, CA 94927

Private collection
Photograph courtesy The Montreal Museum of Fine Arts

A<small>DOLPHE</small>-W<small>ILLIAM</small> B<small>OUGUEREAU</small>
(F<small>RENCH</small>, 1825–1905)

Little Girl Holding Apples, 1895
Oil on canvas, 91.4 x 53.3 cm (36 x 21 in.)

P<small>OMEGRANATE</small>   B<small>OX</small> 6099   R<small>OHNERT</small> P<small>ARK</small>, CA 94927

Private collection
Photograph courtesy Fine Art Photographic
Library Ltd., London

ADOLPHE-WILLIAM BOUGUEREAU
(FRENCH, 1825–1905)

Young Love
Oil on canvas, 101 x 57.8 cm (39¾ x 22¾ in.)

POMEGRANATE BOX 6099 ROHNERT PARK CA 94927

Cummer Museum of Art and Gardens,
Jacksonville, Florida
Bequest of Joseph W. Davin, AG 87.2.1

ADOLPHE-WILLIAM BOUGUEREAU
(FRENCH, 1825–1905)

The Shepherdess, 1889
Oil on canvas, 158.8 x 93.3 cm (62½ x 36¾ in.)

POMEGRANATE BOX 6099 ROHNERT PARK, CA 94927

Gift of Laura A. Clubb, 47.8.82
The Philbrook Museum of Art, Tulsa, Oklahoma

ADOLPHE-WILLIAM BOUGUEREAU
(FRENCH, 1825–1905)

Rest (Le repos), 1879
Oil on canvas, 164.5 x 117.5 cm (64$^{25}/_{32}$ x 46$^{9}/_{32}$ in.)

POMEGRANATE   BOX 6099   ROHNERT PARK CA 94927

ADOLPHE-WILLIAM BOUGUEREAU
(FRENCH, 1825–1905)

Return of Spring (Le printemps), 1886
Oil on canvas, 213.4 x 127 cm (84 x 50 in.)

POMEGRANATE BOX 6099 ROHNERT PARK, CA 94927

Gift of Francis T. B. Martin
Joslyn Art Museum, Omaha, Nebraska

ADOLPHE-WILLIAM BOUGUEREAU
(FRENCH, 1825–1905)

Young Girl, 1886
Oil on canvas, 160.7 x 76.8 cm (63¼ x 30¼ in.)

POMEGRANATE BOX 6099 ROHNERT PARK CA 94927

ADOLPHE-WILLIAM BOUGUEREAU
(FRENCH, 1825–1905)

By the Edge of a Stream, 1875
Oil on canvas, 81.3 x 101.6 cm (32 x 40 in.)

POMEGRANATE   BOX 6099   ROHNERT PARK, CA 94927

Private collection
Photograph courtesy Fine Art Photographic
Library Ltd., London

ADOLPHE-WILLIAM BOUGUEREAU
(FRENCH, 1825–1905)

Mother and Child, 1887
Oil on canvas

POMEGRANATE BOX 6099 ROHNERT PARK CA 94927

Adolphe-William Bouguereau
(French, 1825–1905)

Nymphs and Satyr, 1873
Oil on canvas, 260 x 180 cm (102⅜ x 70⅞ in.)

Pomegranate Box 6099 Rohnert Park CA 94927

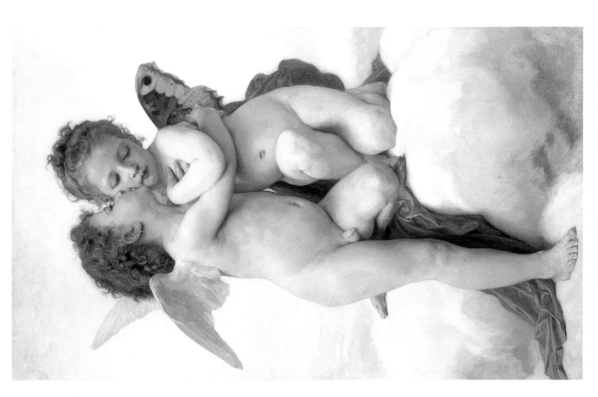

ADOLPHE-WILLIAM BOUGUEREAU
(FRENCH, 1825–1905)

The First Kiss, 1890
Oil on canvas, 119.5 x 71 cm (47 x 28 in.)

POMEGRANATE BOX 6099 ROHNERT PARK, CA 94927

Private collection
Photograph courtesy Christie's Images, London

ADOLPHE-WILLIAM BOUGUEREAU
(FRENCH, 1825–1905)

The Knitting Girl, 1869
Oil on canvas, 144.7 x 99 cm (57 x 39 in.)

POMEGRANATE BOX 6099 ROHNERT PARK CA 94927

Adolphe-William Bouguereau
(French, 1825–1905)

Rest in Harvest, 1865
Oil on canvas, 81.3 x 147.3 cm (32 x 58 in.)

Pomegranate Box 6099 Rohnert Park CA 94927

ADOLPHE-WILLIAM BOUGUEREAU
(FRENCH, 1825–1905)

The Two Sisters, 1877
Oil on canvas, 135 x 78 cm (53½ x 31½ in.)

POMEGRANATE BOX 6099 ROHNERT PARK, CA 94927

Private collection
Photograph courtesy Christie's Images, London

ADOLPHE-WILLIAM BOUGUEREAU
(FRENCH, 1825–1905)

Evening Mood, 1882
Oil on canvas

POMEGRANATE   BOX 6099   ROHNERT PARK CA 94927

National Museum of Art, Havana
Photograph courtesy AKG London

ADOLPHE-WILLIAM BOUGUEREAU
(FRENCH, 1825–1905)

Child at Bath (Petite fille accroupie;
Petite fille assise au bord de l'eau), 1886
Oil on canvas, 83.5 x 61.6 cm (32⅞ x 24¼ in.)

POMEGRANATE BOX 6099 ROHNERT PARK CA 94927

Horace C. Henry Collection, 26.12
Henry Art Gallery, University of Washington
Photograph courtesy Chris Eden

ADOLPHE-WILLIAM BOUGUEREAU
(FRENCH, 1825–1905)

The Young Shepherdess, 1885
Oil on canvas, mounted on board,
157.5 x 72.4 cm (62 x 28½ in.)

POMEGRANATE   BOX 6099   ROHNERT PARK CA 94927

Gift of Mr. and Mrs. Edwin S. Larsen, 1968:082
San Diego Museum of Art

ADOLPHE-WILLIAM BOUGUEREAU
(FRENCH, 1825–1905)

Madonna and Child with Saint John the Baptist, 1882
Oil on canvas, 190.5 x 110.8 cm (75 x 43⅝ in.)

POMEGRANATE BOX 6099 ROHNERT PARK CA 94927

Adolphe-William Bouguereau
(French, 1825–1905)

The Bohemian, 1890
Oil on canvas, 149.9 x 106.7 cm (59 x 42 in.)

Pomegranate Box 6099 Rohnert Park CA 94927

The Christina N. and Swan J. Turnblad
Memorial Fund, 74.33
The Minneapolis Institute of Arts

ADOLPHE-WILLIAM BOUGUEREAU
(FRENCH, 1825–1905)

Spring, 1858
Oil on canvas

POMEGRANATE · BOX 6099 · ROHNERT PARK, CA 94927

ADOLPHE-WILLIAM BOUGUEREAU
(FRENCH, 1825–1905)

Innocence, 1893
Oil on canvas

POMEGRANATE   BOX 6099   ROHNERT PARK CA 94927

Private collection
Photograph courtesy The Bridgeman Art Library, London

ADOLPHE-WILLIAM BOUGUEREAU
(FRENCH, 1825–1905)

The Little Shepherdess, 1891
Oil on canvas, 155.5 x 86.4 cm (61¼ x 34 in.)

POMEGRANATE BOX 6099 ROHNERT PARK, CA 94927

Private collection
Photograph courtesy Christie's Images, London

ADOLPHE-WILLIAM BOUGUEREAU
(FRENCH, 1825–1905)

The Elder Sister
Oil, 55.5 x 45.5 cm (21^{27}/$_{32}$ x 17^{29}/$_{32}$ in.)

POMEGRANATE BOX 6099 ROHNERT PARK CA 94927

POMEGRANATE   BOX 6099   ROHNERT PARK CA 94927

ADOLPHE-WILLIAM BOUGUEREAU
(FRENCH, 1825–1905)
The Elder Sister
Oil, 55.5 x 45.5 cm (21 $^{27}/_{32}$ x 17 $^{29}/_{32}$ in.)

ADOLPHE-WILLIAM BOUGUEREAU
(FRENCH, 1825–1905)

The Captive, 1891
Oil on canvas, 130.8 x 77.5 cm (51½ x 30½ in.)

POMEGRANATE BOX 6099 ROHNERT PARK, CA 94927

Gift of Sidney Spitzer in memory of
General Ceilan M. Spitzer
Toledo Museum of Art

Adolphe-William Bouguereau
(French, 1825–1905)

Temptation, 1880
Oil on canvas, 97 x 130 cm (38³⁄₁₆ x 51³⁄₁₆ in.)

Pomegranate   Box 6099   Rohnert Park CA 94927

The Putnam Dana McMillan Fund and the
M. Knoedler Fund, 74.74
The Minneapolis Institute of Arts

Adolphe-William Bouguereau
(French, 1825–1905)

Young Priestess, 1902
Oil on canvas, 181 x 81 cm (71¼ x 32 in.)

Pomegranate   Box 6099   Rohnert Park CA 94927

Adolphe-William Bouguereau
(French, 1825–1905)

Invading Cupid's Realm, 1892
Oil on canvas, 213.4 x 152.4 cm (84 x 60 in.)

Pomegranate   Box 6099   Rohnert Park CA 94927

ADOLPHE-WILLIAM BOUGUEREAU
(FRENCH, 1825–1905)

The Broken Pitcher, 1891
Oil on canvas, 135.3 x 84.5 cm (53¼ x 33¼ in.)

POMEGRANATE   BOX 6099   ROHNERT PARK CA 94927